I hope you find

is fun, too

Eileen Hobden.

Fun with Weaving

EILEEN HOBDEN

KAYE & WARD · LONDON
in association with Methuen of Australia
and Hicks Smith, New Zealand

Contents

Introduction

In this book you will find ideas for weaving with very simple tools. Some processes need no tools at all, only nimble fingers, and many of the materials recommended for use can be found around the house.

Whether you like to make things you can use, like bags, purses, sandals, cushions and belts, or cheerful hangings just for fun, there are suggestions to start you off.

Weave with wool, cotton, nylon, unspun fleece, handspun wool, beads, raffia, or whatever you can find. You can even 'recycle' strips of material and old jerseys.

This book is meant for beginners. If, as I do, you find weaving really *is* fun, you will be able to learn more of the craft from other books, from weavers, and from keeping your eyes and ears open wherever you travel.

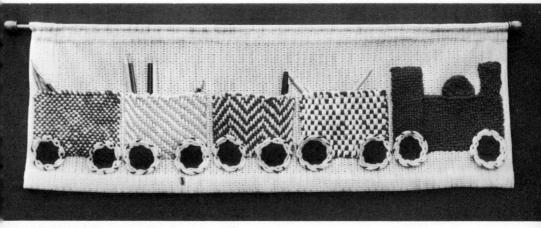

1.   Train hanging — sampler of woven patches.

Finger Weaving – Cords and Plaits

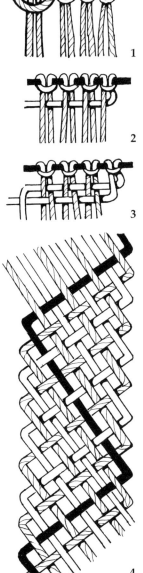

Peruvian Flat Braid

Finger weaving is simple, quick to set up, and needs no loom, so it makes an ideal 'starter'.

In most weaving there are two sets of threads, the *warp*, running lengthwise, and the *weft*, going across and in and out of the warp. In simple braiding there is just one set of strands, with one at a time being woven across the rest, then becoming part of the warp again. Diagrams 2–4 explain how this happens.

Peruvian braids can be woven loosely, so that the strands make a zig-zag pattern, or pulled firmly so that the weft thread is hidden, to give a pattern of diagonal stripes. The open weave is 'springy' and is suitable for hairbands, hatbands, sashes, and for decorating clothes; the firmly woven braids make good belts, bag handles and dog leads. Either can be used in hangings of all kinds, and as a finish for the warp ends of other kinds of weaving.

How to begin

Start with an open weave braid, using thick yarn (heavy knitting yarn or rug wool, for instance) in four different colours. This makes the pattern easy to follow.

The threads need to be secured side by side. A simple method is to attach them to a piece of string, which is then tied to something firm, such as a door handle, a hook on the wall, a chair, or a fence rail.

4

When measuring your threads allow one and a half times the length of the braid you need. If you start by making a hatband or hairband, cut four two metre lengths of thick yarn, of different colours. Bend each in half and attach with a larks head knot (diagram 1) to the holding string, so that there are 8 strands, each a metre long.

Tie the string at a convenient height for working and begin weaving with the strand from one edge, going under and over to the other edge. It doesn't matter whether you start at the left or the right. Do whichever seems natural to you, then always work from the same edge.

As you will see, the braid has a slant to it. If you have a good arrangement of colours, the zig-zag pattern is most attractive. As you weave let the weaving strand stick out to the side until the next thread comes along, then turn the first one down over the next strand. (See diagrams 2 & 3).

To make the diagrams clear the strands are shown very widely spaced; they should be drawn more closely together, but not so tightly that the zig-zag pattern is lost.

After finger weaving the required length, the ends can be finished with a single cord or two thinner cords. Instructions for these appear on pages 10 and 11.

When the holding string is removed the beginning loops can be drawn together neatly, or matching yarn can be threaded through the loops to make cords to match the other end. The ends can then be tied in a knot or a bow to complete a hairband or hatband, or the ends can simply be bound and stitched with matching thread. In the picture on page 9 the belt and matching trimming on the bag were woven in 'Can Can'.

Weaving longer braids

A long warp can be a nuisance because of tangled threads, so avoid this difficulty by weaving a long braid from the middle to one end, then going back to the middle to complete the second half.

Try using several thicknesses of light-weight yarn as a single strand. Mistakes are less likely if each pair of strands is different from the pair on either side, so that it is easy to see which to pick up.

Having cut your threads, find the halfway point and arrange them in order, securing them at the centre on a length of sticky tape. You can then fasten them to a board with bulldog clips

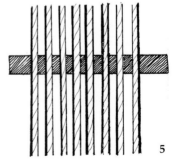

5

or loop them on a length of dowel. A clamp for pressing flowers, or even an old-style tennis racket press, will also hold the strands in order. Loop or tie the second half of the warp to keep it out of the way as you weave the first half.

Vary the design by re-grouping the threads for part of the braid. For instance two strands could be worked as one.

Finish off with corded ends. Here again you may start with a few thick cords, then divide the strands again to finish with a number of tiny cords or plaits.

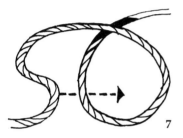

Close weave

By pulling the weft strand tightly, so that it is covered by the warp, a firmly woven braid results. (See colour picture, page 12). If the threads are arranged in pairs, as before, the braid will have narrow diagonal stripes, and will be much narrower than an open weave with the same number of strands.

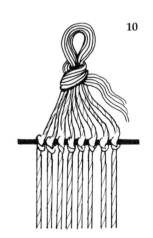

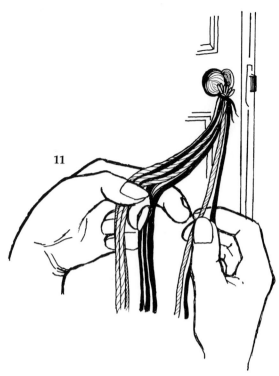

As you will probably want to work with many more strands, this is an opportunity to learn to use the fingers to make a 'shed' so that you can draw the weft across in one movement. This seems awkward at first, but it is worth practising so that it becomes easy, and you will work much more quickly as a result.

Again, it is simplest to start with thick yarn, so set up your threads as before. If you don't want to make a long piece at this stage, work with a short warp – 50 cm for instance – because a collection of short lengths can make an interesting hanging, and nothing need be wasted.

With the strands firmly tied or clamped, hold the warp in the right hand, then transfer the strands, one at a time, to the left hand, placing the first over the index finger, and the next between the index and middle fingers, alternatively, until all the strands are in the left hand. You have made a 'shed', with one thread 'up' and the next 'down'.

Practise transferring the warp from one hand to the other without losing the shed. Now, holding the warp in the left hand, with the fingers of the right hand carefully take the top strand on the extreme left and draw it *through* the shed to the right-hand side.

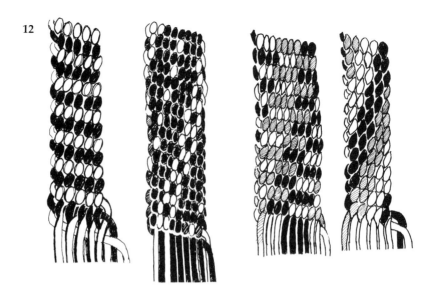

Now you must change the shed, that is, change 'down' threads to up, and vice versa. Holding the warp (in the original shed position) in your right hand, move the first thread, which is now 'down' onto the left index finger, the second between the fingers, and so on, until the warp is in the left hand as before, with the threads in the new shed position. Draw the top left-hand thread through, as before. Working this way seems clumsy at first, but soon the movement becomes easy. Say 'up, down, up, down,' to remind yourself what comes next.

When this form of finger weaving has become familiar, try to vary the effect with stripes of varying width, and experiment with patterns.

A single thread in a contrasting colour makes a dotted line, as the thread comes up in alternate sheds.

If, on each side of a single thread of one colour, there are two threads of another colour, there is the effect of a chain. Using two colours alternately, one dark, then one light, results in crosswise stripes. Some of these variations you will see in the photograph on page 12, and once you have tried, you will be able to plan your own original patterns.

At the end of the book you will find how to use your braids to make them into belts, or bag handles. For a tie belt the ends can be corded or plaited.

Using lightweight yarns you can make original bookmarks in finger-weaving, or you can make a husky belt or luggage strap with string. The possibilities are endless.

Four-strand Cord

This is one of the most useful cords, as it is simple, decorative, firm and hardwearing. A four strand cord of thick heavy strands makes an excellent bag handle, and finer cords can be used to finish braids of all kinds.

When the working method is familiar many colour combinations can be used, but it is simple to learn using two strands in each of two colours. With all four strands held firmly (as when starting a braid) take the two light strands in one hand and the two dark strands in the other hand.

Take the outside strand on the left behind two strands, then back in front of one, to finish as the inside strand in the left hand. (Diagram 13).

Next take the outside right-hand strand similarly behind two and back in front of one. (Diagram 14).

Continue like this, keeping one colour to each hand, saying 'behind two, in front of one' and the movement becomes quick and easy. Finish off by tying two strands round the end of the cord.

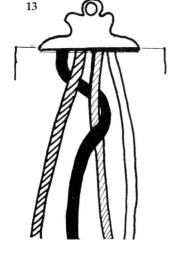

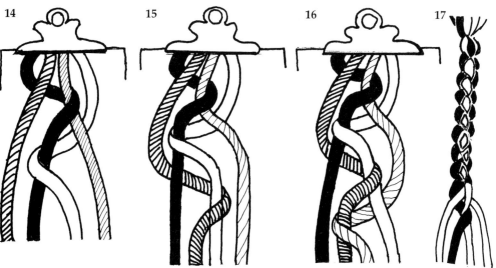

10

If you have to leave a cord unfinished, use a clothes peg or a bulldog clip to hold the strands in the right position, and write a reminder, such as 'black on right, move black next'. The clip will make it clear which is the higher, outside thread at each side.

Five-strand Plait

Most people are familiar with the three strand plait used for braiding hair. The same method can be used for any odd number of strands.

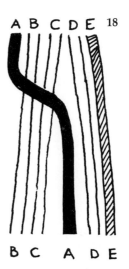

Start with five strands, held side by side. Take the strand from the extreme left over two strands and place it as in diagram 18 between strands C and D. Now take the strand from the extreme right over two strands and place it as in diagram 19 between C and A. Continue like this, taking the outside strand inwards over two strands from each side in turn, as in diagram 20.

The same method can be used for any odd number of strands, so that with seven, the strand goes over three and with nine strands, it goes over four.

Needle Weaving on Simple Frames

A strong wooden frame is necessary for large pieces of weaving, but small items can easily be made using strong cardboard, or the polystyrene trays used for packaging. With a length of sticky tape to strengthen the edges where the holes are made, these small frames last a long time. The smaller sizes (about 130 mm square) are the best to start with, and will make 'patches' about 90 mm square. Later you can try using larger frames, which need more careful handling, as they are inclined to buckle.

By stitching the patches together you can make cushions, pencil cases, purses, cot or pram covers, and just two are needed for a pin cushion or lavender sachet. Patches woven in tabby and a variety of twills will make a sampler to refer to when you are planning larger weaving projects. The train on p. 3 is a sampler and a pencil holder, too.

2. Articles made from woven patches.

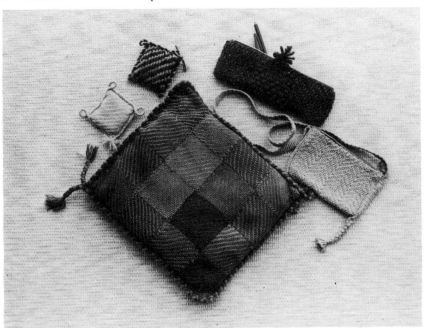

13

Preparing the Frame

The warp (lengthwise) threads go through the loops made by rows of oversewing stitches on two inside edges of the frame, as can be seen from the diagram. When the weaving is finished the foundation stitches are removed, leaving a woven square with neat edges.

To make a square with sides of about 90 mm take a piece of strong cardboard, or a polystyrene tray about 130 mm square and carefully cut out the centre, leaving a border about 20 mm wide.

The holes for the foundation threads are made 5 mm from the inside edge of two opposite sides. Use sticky tape to strengthen those sides, before marking a row of dots. For use with double knitting, make the dots 5 mm apart, or for 'double double' yarn (like Corgi) they should be 10 mm apart.

The foundation loops are made by oversewing through the dots, using a strong smooth yarn, which will be removed when the weaving is finished. Start with a knot at A, and work across through all the dots to B. With another thread start similarly at C and work across to D. Now tie the ends together between B & D, taking the thread at D inside first, and outside first at B.

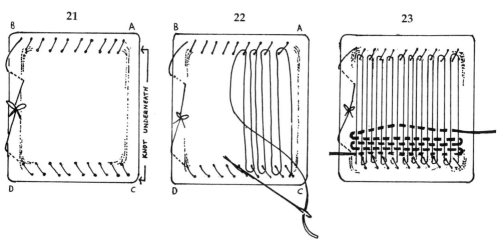

Putting on the warp

Work with the curve of the frame upwards, and using a long thread (about 1½ m of thick yarn, 3 m of double knitting) and a blunt needle, start by tying with a single knot to the first stitch at C. Now thread the

14

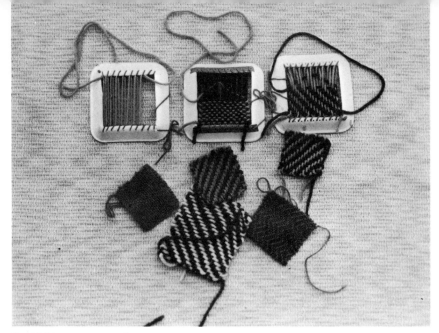

3. Making woven patches.

warp through the first stitch at A, down to the next on the side C to D, and so on, working across to D, where the end is tied with a single knot to secure it. Try not to push the needle through the threads of the foundation loops, or they are more difficult to remove when the work is finished. If a new length of warp has to be joined, tie with a knot near the foundation loops.

Tabby

This is the simplest, firmest weave, working under one and over one, as in darning. Thread your blunt needle with yarn of a similar thickness to the warp, and beginning at one corner, work under and over, across the warp, as in the diagram. Push the weft (across) thread down with your needle, or with a fork or piece of comb, trying to space the weft to match the warp. Be careful not to pull tightly. Let the weft lie in a curve before pushing it down. Continue until the warp is covered (the last few 'shots' of weft may be rather difficult to fit in) then carefully remove the foundation threads, taking care not to cut the weaving. You should have a neatly woven square, with just a few ends which can be used for stitching the squares together.

Twill

One of the easiest weaving variations is a 'two and two twill', going under two and over two, moving along one warp thread with each shot so that you get a diagonal pattern. This shows up well if the weft is in a contrasting colour to the warp.

To work the twill, set up the warp as before and go 'under 2, over 2' as shown in the diagram.

If the number of warp threads can be divided evenly by four the next three shots will be:
(2) under 1, then over 2 under 2, finishing under 1
(3) over 2, under 2
(4) over 1, then under 2 over 2, finishing over 1.

If you have a number of warp threads which is a multiple of four with 2 over, the sequence will be
(1) Under 2, over 2, finishing under 2
(2) Over 1, then under 2, over 2, finishing under 1
(3) Over 2, under 2, finishing over 2
(4) Under 1, then over 2, under 2, finishing over 1
Repeat from the first shot.

Finish with a second or fourth shot, so that you go through the warp loops at the end, and remove the foundation threads as before.

Once you understand the way twill develops, you can work variations, like zig-zags, sloping first one way, then the other. Be careful to go round the outside thread each time.

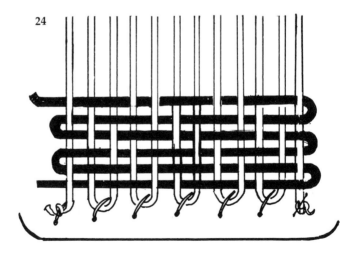

Hopsack

This is a basket weave, going under two and over two, like a double version of tabby. As the diagram shows, the second shot is like the first, except that the weft must go round the warp thread at the edge, to hold the first shot in position. If this is not done, you will undo the first shot. The third and fourth shots are worked in a similar way, but start over 2 instead of under 2.

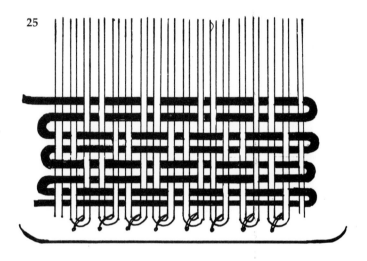

Larger squares or oblongs

Larger frames made from polystyrene or card need to be strengthened with tape on all four sides, or they are liable to buckle under the strain. Practise first with small squares, then try larger shapes. Finer yarn can be used with two thicknesses, or on a closer warp, and if you have a frame of really tough card with holes punched for foundation threads, thick rug wool can be used effectively.

Joining squares

If you have woven the squares evenly, there will be the same number of loops along each edge, so it is easy to join them together, taking the needle through a loop from one square, then from the next, making sure the seam will lie flat.

Spinning

Handspun wool will add interest to your weaving, as even your first knobbly efforts will give a really individual touch to your work.

To make a start you simply need a piece of dowel, a small potato, and some oddments of fleece. If you pick up wool in the fields in summer, choose the freshly shed pieces, with natural oil in them, rather than the dry old bits from last year. Avoid very short fleece, too, as anything less than 4 cm is difficult for a beginner to spin.

Making your Spindle

Having gathered your wool, make your spindle. Take a 30 cm (1 ft) length of dowel, sharpen one end to a point, and push it through the potato, so that about 2 cm (¾ in) protrudes. Round off the other end of the stick, so that it is comfortable to hold, and make an upward sloping notch about 2½ cm (1 in) from the top.

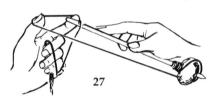

Spinning

Tie one end of a 40 cm (16 in approx.) length of ready spun wool onto the spindle just above the potato, then take the yarn down round the point, and up to the top, holding it in the notch with a half hitch.

Take a small handful of fleece and 'tease' it, that is, open it up so that grit and twigs fall out. Tease out the cut end first, then the tips. If you can finish with the fibres lying more or less parallel they will draw out into a continuous thread more easily.

With the spindle ready to pick up, hold the teased fleece in the left hand, and with the right hand start drawing out fibres, holding the main bunch firmly between the left forefinger and thumb. Overlap the drawn

out fibres on the last few inches of wool on the
spindle, and, still holding firmly with the left
hand, twist the spindle with the right hand,
turning it clockwise. Stand so that the
spindle can move freely. The 'spin' will now
run up from the spun wool to the drawn out
fibres.

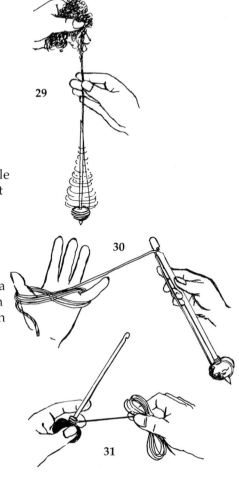

29

30

31

While the spindle is still spinning, move the
right hand up to the left hand, move the left
hand back a little, and draw out more threads
between your two hands. As long as the spindle
continues to turn clockwise, go on drawing out
a little at a time and letting the 'spin' run up.
Use the right hand to give an extra turn to the
spindle when necessary. You will soon sense
when it begins to slow down. Don't let it stop,
or the wool will untwist and break.

If this is too much to think about at once, let a
friend watch the spindle, giving it an extra turn
when necessary, so that you can concentrate on
drawing out fibres, then letting the 'spin' run
up to the left hand. Later you can combine all
the movements.

Winding On

When the yarn is so long that you want to stop
and wind it on, do not let it slacken, or it will
twist back on itself. Wind from the fleece end
onto your finger and thumb in a 'figure 8' until
you reach the spindle, then unhook from the notch, and the point at the
bottom. Wind neatly onto the spindle just above the potato, leaving
enough to go round the point, and half-hitch into the notch as before. It
pays to wind on neatly and evenly, keeping the weight of the wool low on
the spindle, as this helps the balance, and makes the ball of wool easy to
remove when it is finished.

32

Don't worry about lumps and bumps. If you get a continuous yarn of
any kind the first time you try you are doing well. Remember to keep the
spindle spinning, and gradually you will work to an easy rhythm, drawing out just the right amount for the thickness of thread you need.

Skeining, Washing and using your wool

When you feel the spindle is getting too heavy to work comfortably, take off the ball of spun wool. It should slide off easily. Keep a short length of it to start off again on the spindle, and, using the backs of two chairs, make the rest of the wool into a skein. Tie it with oddments of yarn in several places, then wash it gently, without twisting or wringing, in soapy water, rinsing several times. The water may be as hot as is comfortable for your hands, and the rinsing water gradually cooler, but don't subject it to sudden changes of temperature. Roll in a towel, then hang it away from direct heat to dry off.

There is, of course, much more to learn about spinning, and far the best way is to watch an expert at work, whether at a wheel or a simple spindle. Spinning can be a fascinating hobby in itself.

You will be able to borrow books from your local library telling you how to dye your wool, using onion skins and weeds from the garden. If you are lucky enough to spin the wool of a Jacob sheep, you will have a range of different shades from white or cream through greys or browns to black or dark brown. The top of the stool in the photograph on page 20 is 'random' spun Jacob, and is 'first attempt' spinning.

4. Stool top from beginner's random spinning of Jacob wool.

Making and using a Wooden Frame Loom

Making your Loom

A simple frame loom is easily made with a few lengths of wood, screws, nails, cuphooks and dowelling. The frame used for most of the weaving shown in this book is 45 cm × 35 cm, with a width of 30 cm between the hooks, but any strong rectangular frame can be adapted. Later, you can make, or buy a loom of the size and type which suits you best.

Having cut the wood to size, rub it smooth and give it a finishing coat (polyurethane varnish, for instance) before screwing the parts together as shown in diagram 34. Wool catches on any rough edges, so a smooth finish is important for efficiency as well as appearance.

The reed, which keeps the warp evenly spaced, is not fastened to the frame. So that the base of the reed does not split, have holes drilled to take the nails, which should be accurately spaced 1 cm apart. A good glue will help to fix them.

Flat pieces of wood, or old rulers, can be made into shuttles by cutting V or U shaped notches at the ends.

A flat stick with a hole each end to take a length of string, makes the shed stick. Tie the string through one hole; the other end will be tied when the shed stick is threaded through the warp.

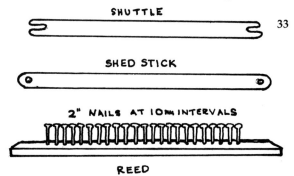

SHUTTLE

33

SHED STICK

2" NAILS AT 10mm INTERVALS

REED

Having cut the dowel for the end rods, hold them in place on the hooks with doubled lengths of string, looped round one rod and tied to the other.

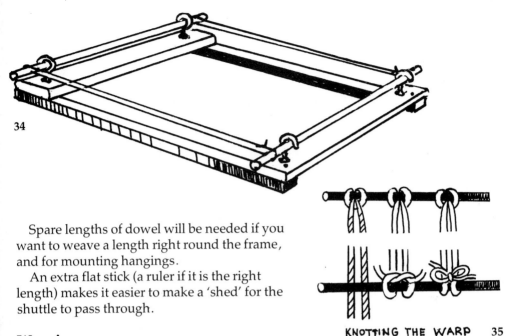

34

Spare lengths of dowel will be needed if you want to weave a length right round the frame, and for mounting hangings.

An extra flat stick (a ruler if it is the right length) makes it easier to make a 'shed' for the shuttle to pass through.

Warping

Use strong, smooth yarn for the warp. It has to stand up to tension and constant lifting and rubbing, so soft fluffy yarns are unsuitable. Save those for the weft.

The warp is stretched between the two dowels in the hooks. For a first effort use a heavy cotton, like dishcloth cotton, or a firmly spun knitting yarn of double knitting thickness.

Decide on the width you wish to work – it isn't necessary to use the full width of the frame. For your first trial, work with two warp threads in each space ('dent') of the reed. The warp threads should be cut to twice the distance between the end rods, plus half a metre, as the warp threads ('ends') are put on in pairs.

Place the reed across the frame, and, starting in the centre, fasten a doubled warp thread onto the end bar with a larks head knot, as shown in diagram 35. Take one end each side of the middle nail of the reed, over the other end rod, bringing one end up each side of the warp threads and tie with a single knot, which will be adjusted for tension and finished as a double knot when the warp threads are all in place. Continue to tie on the rest of the warp, working from the centre outwards, so that there are two threads in each dent of the reed.

23

SIDE VIEW SHOWING SHED STICK

SIDE VIEW SHOWING SHED STICK & RULER

36

Now gently place your hand across the warp, so that you can feel any loose threads. Adjust the tension where necessary, by pulling on the half knots without untying, then when the tension is even, tie the second half of the knots, again working outwards from the centre.

Near the end where you have just tied the knots, work the shed stick under one thread and over one across the warp, counting a double thread as one at each edge.

Take the string, which is tied to one end of the stick, over the warp, and tie to the other end, then push the stick back close to the knots.

Turn the loom so that the shed stick is away from you, and it is ready for you to start weaving.

Beginning to weave

Experiment with all kinds of yarn for the weft, which need not be as strong as the warp. Fine yarns beat down closely, to cover the warp, but when crossed with thick weft threads, the warp is visible. Try strips of leather, ribbon, or cloth, as well as wool of all kinds. Handspun yarns, particularly your first knobbly efforts, can give an interesting texture to an otherwise plain piece of weaving.

Wind yarn onto your shuttle, but do not overfill it, or it will be difficult to push through the 'shed'. Turn the shed stick onto one edge and move it forward, towards the reed. Pass the shuttle through the space ('shed') made in this way, in front of the reed, leaving an end of weft hanging, and push the shot close to the end bar near you, using a fork or the reed to beat it back. Check the width with the reed, to make sure the threads are evenly spaced on the bar.

24

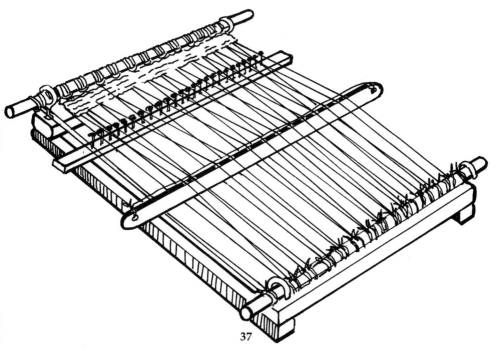

37

Now, using the flat stick or ruler, make the next shed by lifting the alternate warp threads – up instead of down, down instead of up – turning the stick on edge to open the shed. Pass the shuttle through the shed, and beat down the weft as before. Be careful not to pull the weft tightly across. Lay it in a curve to allow for the 'take-up' of interlacing with the warp. You have now worked two shots, one through the shed made by the shed stick, the other picked up with the loose stick. Remember that the shed stick stays in place all the time. Push it back out of the way when finding the second shed.

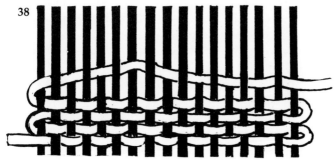

38

TIGHTEN HERE

Carry on weaving in this way, beating down evenly as you go. If, after a few shots, the weft does not lie in a straight line, the warp tension may be uneven. Look at the diagram, and check the tension of the warp. Where the weft is not beating evenly, loosen the knots concerned, pull on the ends to match the tension of the rest of the warp, and complete the ties as before.

When changing to a new weft, first finish the one you are using by going round the outside warp thread and back into the same shed for 2 cm. Join the new weft from the opposite edge, taking the end back into the shed to hold it firmly.

Take care to keep the warp to its full width. If the weft is pulled too tightly, apart from making the edges uneven, the outside threads will be put under too much strain when the reed is moved up and down the warp.

On your first piece of weaving, try out different colours and textures, so that you have a useful sampler to refer to later.

To insert a shot of unspun fleece, tease it out somewhat and roll it between the hands to the thickness required, then push it into the shed carefully using your fingers to help it into place. If you want it to stand out even more, pull up a little fleece between the threads of the warp.

Strips of leather, suede, or ribbon can be pushed into place in a similar way, using the fingers to keep the strip flat. Strips of cloth can be inserted as a flat ribbon or pushed down hard.

When you want to finish off your weaving, thread a needle with smooth yarn, and, with the work still on the frame, oversew into the last two shots of weft.

To make a hanging, the larks head knots can be left in place on the dowel or loosened sufficiently to transfer to another rod. Untie the knots at the other end and finish with plaits, cords, or knotted fringe.

You may oversew and fringe both ends, to make a mat or sampler.

5. Bag with weft of oddments of wool, leather, suede and fur fabric.

Chaining and Soumak

These are two useful weaves which do not need a shed, but are worked with the warp flat. Both give a raised effect.

Chaining, as its name implies, is similar to the chain stitch worked in embroidery or crochet. Apart from making a raised stripe, it helps to space the warp evenly.

After a shot of plain weaving, take the weft underneath the warp, across to the other side. Chaining uses at least three times as much yarn as an ordinary shot of weft, so make sure there is sufficient weft available.

If the warp is widely spaced, it is easy to chain using the fingers, but with a close warp a crochet hook will help.

Make a loop, lay it over the first warp thread, and draw the weft through the loop from the next space. Work across like this, enclosing each warp thread in one link of the chain. See diagram 40. At the end, thread the weft yarn (or shuttle and yarn) through the last loop to hold the chain.

27

Soumak is related to stemstitch or backstitch in embroidery, going over two threads and back under one. Two rows above each other, facing opposite ways, looks like a chain. (Diagram 41).

Both chaining and soumak can be pushed into position after working, either close to the previous weft, or on a curve, for special effects.

6. Chaining and soumak on reverse of bag illustrated on page 27.

Weaving a double length

Your loom can easily be adapted to take a warp almost twice the length of the frame. With the holding strings in place between the rods, use two lengths of string to attach an extra dowel rod. Double the strings and fasten with larks head knots to the ends of the front rod. Knot the double strings about 2 cm from the rod, then tie on the new dowel, as in the diagram below. Tie new holding strings from the new rod, underneath the loom to the rod at the other end of the frame.

The warp threads will now go from the newly fixed rod, under the loom, over the rod at the far end, through the reed to the third rod. Cut double warp lengths as before, measuring right round the loom this time and allowing extra length for tying on.

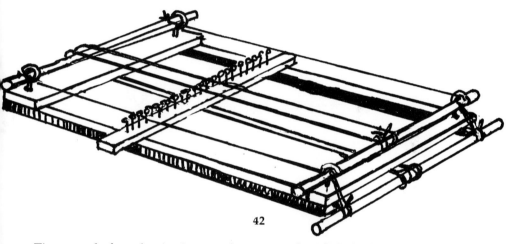

42

Tie on as before, beginning on the new rod with larks head knots, working from the centre outwards, and adding an extra thread at each edge so that you have double threads for the selvedge.

Put the shed stick in place behind the reed, and weaving in the usual way, continue until you need more space to make a good shed. Now slacken off the ties between the end rods sufficiently to move the woven part towards you so that the additional cloth rod goes under the loom. When the work is in a convenient position to carry on, tighten the strings again and put an extra dowel between the hooks. Continue weaving, moving the work round again when necessary. Eventually the warp rod will reach the hooks at the top of the loom and the work can be finished off in the usual way.

7. Double length ready to be moved round loom.

8. Double length after moving round.

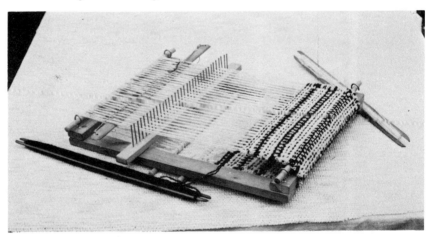

Weaving Cloth in an even Tabby

You will have noticed that a widely spaced warp is covered by the weft, unless the weft is very thick. To weave an even tabby, with equal amounts of warp and weft showing, the dentage (ends per cm/in) must be adjusted according to the thickness of the yarn.

30

44a.   Widely spaced warp – INCORRECT

43.   Even tabby – CORRECT

Wind some of the yarn round a ruler, pushing the coil up closely. Count how many thicknesses there are to the cm. With heavy knitting wool it will be about 8, so, allowing for the weft to interlace the warp, 4 ends per cm should weave to an even tabby.

As the warp shows in the finished work, you can now plan a pattern of lengthwise stripes, which with matching stripes in the weft will result in a pattern of squares. A striped warp is just as easy to put on as a plain one, particularly if it is planned with even numbers of each colour, so that the warp is knotted to the end rod in twos, as before.

Try stripes of contrasting thickness, or texture, as well as colour. In the bags illustrated on pages 44 and 60 the contrasting warp threads are of the same knitting cotton (Lyric) but in double thickness. Remember warp yarns need to be strong, to withstand tension and friction, and see what interesting oddments you can find to add to the warp.

44b.   Widely spaced weft – INCORRECT

The weft can be worked plain, to show lengthwise stripes from the warp, it can match the warp, or be quite different, but for an even tabby the thickness should be the same.

When using two shuttles in turn for check patterns, more care must be taken of the selvedges. The colour not being used may be carried up the side for a short distance, but if the stripes are widely spaced it is better to finish off after each stripe, weaving the end in.

As both warp and weft are part of the pattern,

32

even beating is very important. Any wavy lines will be very obvious. Check the tension of the warp after weaving a short distance, and tighten or slacken where necessary. Measure the number of shots of weft per cm/in too, and keep it the same throughout.

Continuous Warp

Instead of cutting separate warp threads, the warp can be made from a continuous length. Wind the yarn into a ball which will go between the frame and the end rod, tie the end of the yarn to one rod, take it under the rod at the opposite end, back under the first rod, and so on, tying to the rod again at the end. A shorter length can be woven by tying an extra dowel to one of the end bars, using strings adjusted to a suitable length.

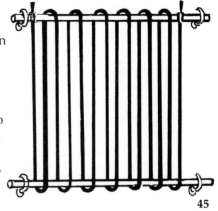

45

Put the shed stick and reed in place as usual, and begin by chaining across the warp.

It is possible to make a neat edge at the beginning when using an extra dowel. After weaving a few shots slip off one of the strings between the new dowel and the end rod, slide off the short length of weaving, and replace the string on the dowel. Now, with a needle and string, or strong yarn, start by tying the string to the dowel, then go through a loop of the weaving, round the dowel, through the next loop, and so on across the warp, finishing by tying to the dowel. Push the weaving down close to the rod, and adjust the tension on the strings. When the weaving is finished, the holding thread can be removed, leaving a neat edge. If, at the end of the weaving, the weft is pushed down particularly close, after the rod has been removed the weft can be pushed up to fill the loops in the warp. The result is a neatly finished piece of weaving, which can quickly be made into a purse, or pencil case, for instance. The neck purse on page 40 was woven on a continuous warp.

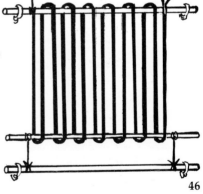

46

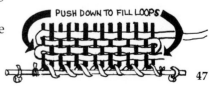

PUSH DOWN TO FILL LOOPS

47

33

Bead Weaving

Since bead weaving has regained its popularity, there are several bead looms available, some quite inexpensive. Before investing in a special loom, however, try bead weaving using your wooden frame. Use whatever beads you have – anything from fine embroidery beads to evenly sized wooden, plastic or glass necklace beads will do.

9. Necklaces in bead weaving.

Any pattern worked out in squares, as for cross stitch, embroidered tapestry, or Fair Isle knitting can be adapted for beads. Draw it out on squared paper, so that it is easy to follow.

If you are using small beads, you will need a strong, fine warp, such as linen thread, or Coats' Drima, but with large beads a smooth 3 or 4 ply strong knitting yarn works well, as the colour forms part of the pattern and the ends can be finished as finger-woven cords. A warp of shirring elastic makes a bracelet easy to push over the hand.

Warping the frame loom

On your wooden frame loom the length of the bead weaving strip is limited, so anything you make must be planned accordingly. After a little practice on the frame, a beaded belt can be made by fixing the warp threads direct to the buckle bar, and weaving without a loom, holding the warp as in finger weaving. Bead looms have rollers so that any reasonable length can be woven.

35

Begin with a simple pattern, with just a few beads in each row. Each bead goes between two warp threads, so 8 warp threads are needed for a band 7 beads wide.

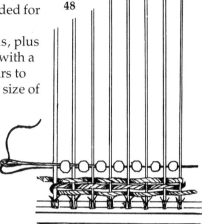

48

Cut the warp threads in double lengths, plus the length required for tying on, and fix with a larks head knot to the end rod. Tie in pairs to the second rod. Space the warp to fit the size of the beads.

Weaving

The thread used for the weft must be fine enough to go twice through the beads, so choose a strong thread of suitable thickness.

To help in the even spacing of the warp, you may work a few shots of weft with an oddment of yarn, to be removed later, or you may need a short length of weaving without beads to help in finishing off your woven band.

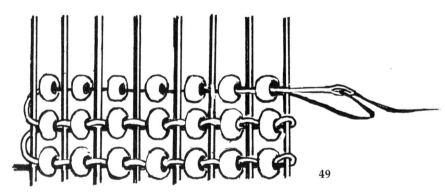

49

Choose a needle which easily passes through the beads. Tie the end of the weft to the outside warp thread, leaving a few inches hanging. Now with the needle, pick up the beads needed for the first row of the pattern, in the correct order. Take the weft underneath the warp, and push the beads up into position between the warp threads. Going *over* the warp, push the needle through the beads again, to hold the beads in position.

Place your beads in saucers, or shallow dishes, so that it is easy to pick up a bead on the needle, and follow the pattern chosen, marking off the rows completed.

If you need to join in a new thread, first finish off the old one by working back through two rows of beads, then start the new thread through the last completed row before resuming the pattern. If the beads are large, a new thread can be knotted to the old one, and the knot will be out of sight inside a bead.

When planning a necklace which is divided into two halves above the pattern at the base, have an equal number of warp threads at the beginning. The pattern starts with an odd number of beads, then when the warp divides there is a space above the centre bead.

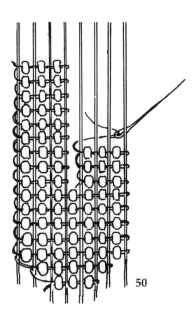

50

Finishing

If the necklace is long enough to go over the head without a fastening, the warp threads can be knotted together in pairs, one from each end of the necklace, then the warp ends can be glued to the underside and covered with a piece of ribbon. (It helps to have somebody to hold the two ends while you tie the knots.)

With large beads, the warp ends can be worked into the beads one at a time to hold the join firm. (See the bracelet on page 31.)

A heavy warp can be braided and tied, adding extra threads through the last row of beads to make a solid cord. (See the necklaces on pages 31 and 35.)

51

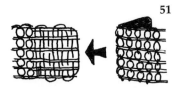

52

37

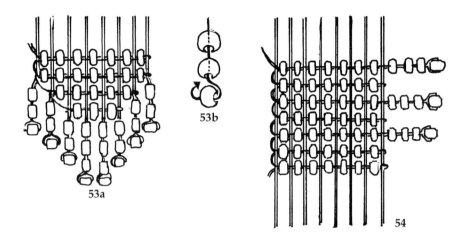

53b

53a

54

Finer threads can be woven into a tab at each end, darning in the warp ends. Stick one end underneath and attach Velcro as a fastening. Necklace ring bolt fasteners are suitable for a fine warp.

The woven ends may be stitched or glued between two lengths of ribbon or leather, or the whole beaded band may be mounted on ribbon or leather for a choker necklace or belt.

Extra beads, threaded onto the warp ends, make a good finish to a necklace. See that the threads are secured into the woven band after working back through all but the last bead on the fringe.

Similarly, beads are added as a fringe along one side, by threading them onto the weft during the weaving, as in the choker of large beads on page 35.

Tapestry

Tapestry is a closely beaten plain weave where the warp is completely covered. Depending on the materials used, the same technique can produce a heavy fabric, suitable for a rug, or a finely detailed tapestry picture.

The warp has to take a lot of pressure, so it must be strong.

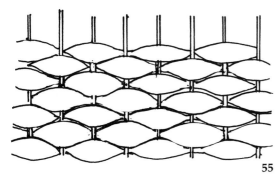

55

Simple Tapestry

Begin with a very simple design, using two colours of the same weight of yarn, before tackling anything ambitious. A widely spaced knitting cotton warp – 2 ends per cm – and heavy weight knitting yarn or medium rug yarn for the weft, will be easy to handle.

Effective patterns can be made with blocks and stripes. Working alternate shots in two colours gives vertical stripes. After 3 or 4 shots of each colour, work 2 successive shots with one colour, then alternate again and you get a pattern of squares.

Be careful, when using two shuttles, to keep neat edges, crossing under or over the second weft at the edge to keep the pattern correct.

10. Simple tapestry patterns.

11. Simple tapestry on bag and neck purse. Purse has strap in finger weaving.

You may wish to work your first piece of tapestry entirely in stripes and checks. Try out different colour combinations, using only two at the same time, to see what effects you can create.

The striped cushion in 'Can Can' on page 9, the small bag in handspun wool and the purse beside it were worked this way.

Shapes in Tapestry

To make a tapestry picture you will need to work with two or more colours in the same shot, and colour changes may be interlocked, dove-tailed, or 'slit', as you will see from the diagrams.

The 'slit' method is the simplest, and is suitable for sloping lines, or very short vertical

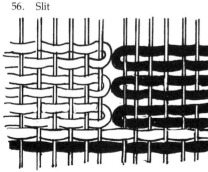

56. Slit

lines, but a long vertical slit weakens the fabric. The interlocked join needs to be worked carefully to avoid a ridge, and the dovetail gives a slightly wavy outline. By trying each method you will find what suits your purpose best. Where the colour change moves diagonally the 'slit' join is the simplest, and is quite strong.

It takes practice to work a tapestry to a detailed plan, so start with a random, abstract pattern experimenting in making shapes. You may find you can work best with small shuttles, or with 'butterflies' of yarn made by winding round the fingers. Try varying the design with yarns of different textures but of similar weight. Use a fork as a beater, but check length and width with the reed.

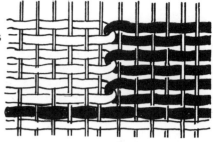

57.   Interlocked

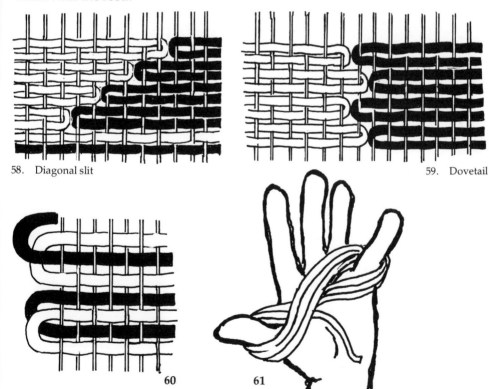

58.   Diagonal slit

59.   Dovetail

60

61

41

12. Hanging with various tapestry techniques and Ghiordes knots.

Knots

Pattern can be introduced into your tapestry by working knots into the design. The same technique is used to make pile rugs. By joining squares made on your simple frame you can even make a full-size rug!

Each knot (known as a Ghiordes knot) is worked over two warp threads. Diagram 62 shows how they are worked. The length of pile can vary according to the effect you want in your design. Pull on the two ends to secure the knot, and then work several rows in plain weave. The longer the pile, the more plain shots are worked between the rows of knots.

Knots take up much more space than plain weaving, so put in extra shots of weft alongside the knots, to level up a row. If you want an all-over design of knots, still leave a border of plain weaving over a few warp threads at each edge, and here put in the extra shots of weft to give a firm edge.

On the sampler illustrated on page 42 the knots were made from strips

42

62

cut from an old machine-knitted jersey. Some of the plain shots were worked in the same fabric, the rest of the weft being medium-weight rug wool. The green and orange hanging on page 34 is worked with a combination of double knitting and boucle yarn, and Ghiordes knots form the fringe.

Open Warp design

Obviously the warp must be covered to withstand wear as a bag, cushion, or rug, but hangings can be made using tapestry techniques, leaving part of the warp unwoven. The Christmas tree hanging on page 31 and two of the mini pictures on page 45 were worked this way.

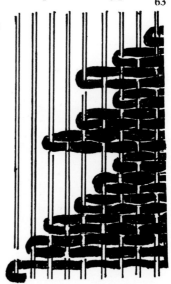

63

As the warp is part of the pattern its colour is important. The finished hanging may be mounted on a matching background, or one of another colour, with the open warp giving a pattern of stripes.

It helps to weave a solid base to the hanging, to set the spacing, and the addition of a bar of wood or metal, or heavy beads, will keep the warp at full stretch on the finished hanging. Beads can be added to the warp ends as part of the pattern. The 'candles' on the tree are cut from drinking straws.

Lines of chaining or soumak can be set in curves which will hold their position on an open warp.

43

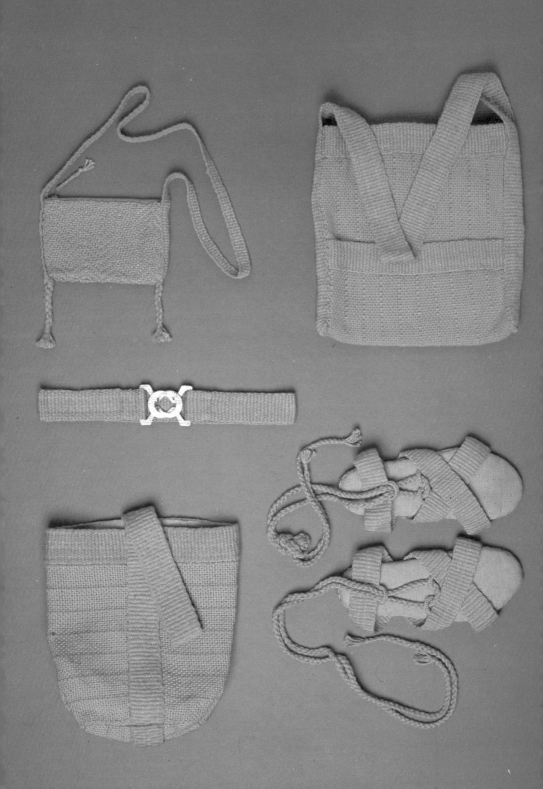

13. Mini-pictures.

Mini Pictures

Small tapestry pictures can be made with ready-made frames, by weaving them on card or polystyrene, with the centre cut away. Strengthen the underside with sticky tape before marking dots, 3mm or 5mm ($^1/_{10}$ in or $^1/_8$ in) apart, and 5mm ($^1/_4$ in) from the inside edge of two opposite sides.

With a needle threaded with smooth, strong, fairly fine yarn, and starting with a knot on the underside, work from end to end as in the diagram, working the end of the yarn into the stitches at the back.

Your design can be sketched on paper and taped to the back of the frame, or you can work 'free-hand', following a sketch. Make the design simple, and use lightweight yarns, as anything heavy will be a strain on the frame, and too clumsy to give detail to your picture.

Any tapestry technique, including knots, and open warp, can be used, and for those who like working on a small scale this is an ideal way of producing something original in 'pocket' size.

64

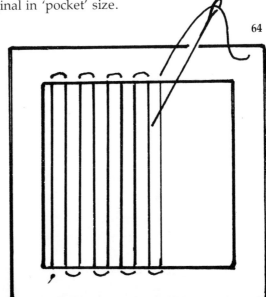

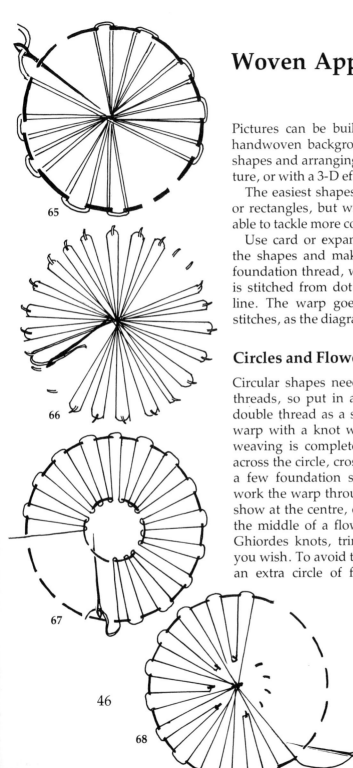

Woven Appliqué

Pictures can be built up on a ready-made or handwoven background, by weaving separate shapes and arranging them, either flat, as a picture, or with a 3-D effect.

The easiest shapes are those based on circles or rectangles, but with a few trials you will be able to tackle more complicated outlines.

Use card or expanded polystyrene, drawing the shapes and making outlines with dots. A foundation thread, which will be removed later is stitched from dot to dot, following the outline. The warp goes through the foundation stitches, as the diagrams show.

Circles and Flowers

Circular shapes need an odd number of warp threads, so put in an extra thread, or work a double thread as a single one. Begin a circular warp with a knot which can be cut when the weaving is complete. Work from side to side across the circle, crossing at the centre, or make a few foundation stitches in the middle and work the warp through them. As the warp will show at the centre, choose a colour suitable for the middle of a flower, or make the centre of Ghiordes knots, trimmed down to the length you wish. To avoid too much bulk in the centre, an extra circle of foundation threads can be

65

66

67

68

69

46

worked, as shown in diagram 68. To give a curve to a flower shape, weave it with a hole in the middle, (diagram 67), then gather round the hole before stitching to the background.

Flower petals can be woven by dividing the warp into small sections. This will be seen in the 'basket of flowers' picture on page 56.

Leaves

Leaves can have radiating 'veins', or two foundation stitches at the top and bottom can hold the warp threads, which are then drawn apart to weave the leaf to the shape required. The photograph shows how the leaves of the hollyhock on the back cover were made.

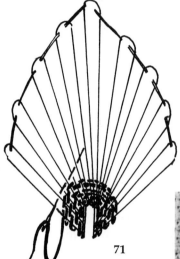

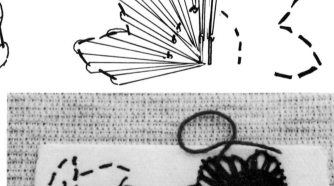

14.   Weaving hollyhock leaves.

15. Weaving a tree.

Trees

Bare trees can be worked by making a warp the full height of the tree. Begin to weave across the whole trunk, (let it grow narrower as it goes up), then divide the warp, and re-divide to make branches. Return to the unwoven warp when one branch is completed, and continue until the tree is ready to detach from the card. Pull it into shape and stitch to the background with the branches arranged as you wish. (See the 'rabbit' picture on page 56.)

Other shapes

Buildings can be built up from simple shapes. Raffia will make good haystacks and thatched roofs.

Animals can be made to look more realistic by padding them slightly when they are stitched into place.

Knots can be used for thatched roofs or green trees, and lines of chain or soumak give the right texture for a basket.

Generally the weft needs to be fairly fine, especially where the warp threads lie close together.

Norwegian Braid

A hole and slot heddle is a useful addition to your weaving equipment. With it you can make Norwegian braid for belts, bag-handles, luggage straps, dog-leads and children's reins, or more lightweight bands to decorate clothes, cushions or curtains. Stitched side by side the braids make attractive purses, bags and pencil cases. Braids can be woven with slits to make buttonhole bands or guitar straps.

The heddle

Hole and slot heddles can be bought ready-made or you can make your own. Choose lightweight, strong materials. The two illustrated have frames of formica, with the slats on one being made from 'lolly' sticks, and plant support sticks make the other.

As the warp is drawn closely together the heddle should be made with the slots just wide enough for the warp threads to pass through, and the holes drilled through the middle of the slats should be just big enough to thread with warp threads, using a needle or hook. A heddle with 15 to 20 slats will be sufficient at first.

16. Hole and slot heddles.

Planning Patterns

All the pattern in these braids comes from the arrangement of the warp, as, except at the edges, the weft is completely covered. There are two sheds, when the 'hole' and 'slot' threads come up alternatively.

A single thread in a contrasting colour makes a dotted line, two side by side make a slightly wavy line, and three side by side a chain effect. Two pairs of threads with one of contrasting colour between gives the 'small flower' pattern, and alternate dark and light threads make stripes across the braid.

After a little practice you will devise your own patterns, as with finger-weaving. Draw a diagram on squared paper, and if you want a symmetrical pattern, begin in the centre and work outwards, matching the pattern. Have the edge threads the same colour as the weft.

17. Patterns in Norwegian B

Setting up the warp

When measuring the warp, allow ½ m longer than the finished braid required. Use a firmly spun, strong yarn which will stand up to the pull during weaving. For an end bar use a strong stick with holes bored at each end for waist ties, or use a short length of hose or tube, with the waist tie threaded through. A 6 in (15 cm) length of hose or stick will be quite long enough.

You can hitch doubled lengths to the end bar or tie single threads separately.

To put on the warp, tie the end bar to the back of a chair, which is pushed up to a table. On the opposite edge of the table place the heddle flat between two books, so that the holes are just beyond the table edge, as in diagram 74. The warp is threaded in the correct order, working outwards from the centre, taking each thread from the stick, or tube, across the table through the correct hole or slot. To make a thick braid, double threads can be used as one strand. When all the warp has been threaded through the heddle, gather the ends together, pull them firmly, 'combing' with the heddle to make sure there are no loose threads, then knot the ends together. Fasten the knotted end to a hook, window catch, door knob, table leg, or something similar.

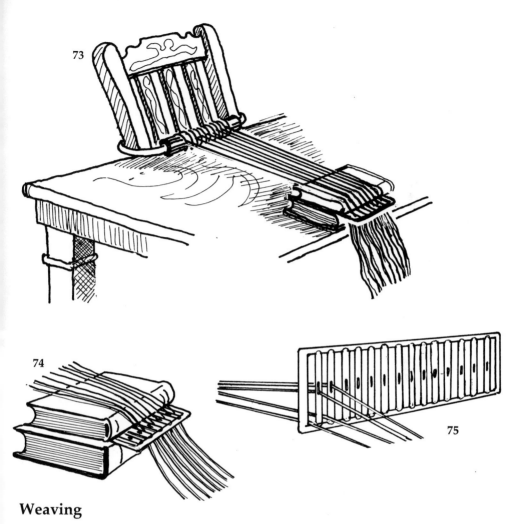

Weaving

Fill a small shuttle with weft yarn, and tie the end bar round your waist, or round the back of your chair. Old nylons, or a length of braid, slotted through the piece of hose will be more comfortable than string if you tie the 'loom' to your waist.

Sit in a position which will hold the warp tight, and you will find the heddle moves up and down easily. Raise the heddle, use your hand or a flat stick to 'clear' the shed, and pass the weft through, leaving a short length hanging. Lower the heddle for the second shed, clear with your hand, and insert the weft as before, beating well back.

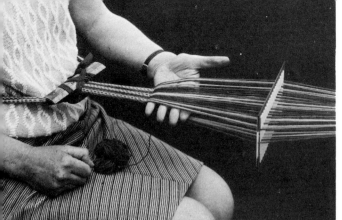

18. Weaving Norwegian braid, (part rolled on and tied to front bar).

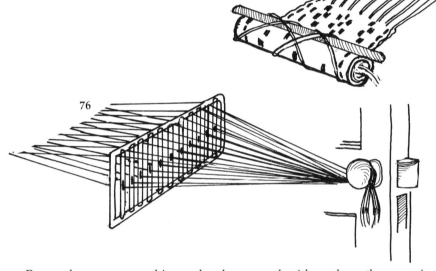

Remember you are making a closely woven braid, so draw the warp in to cover the weft. Continue to weave in this way, keeping the edges neat, and beating as evenly as possible.

If you are weaving with the work tied to your waist, as the piece of weaving grows it will become difficult to reach. Untie the waistband, roll the woven braid round the end bar, and with a string or braid tie another stick over the first one to hold the rolled-up braid in place. Now continue.

You may prefer to tie both ends of the warp to two fixtures at a suitable distance apart, so that you can move along as you work.

A long settle with arms makes a good 'stand', or some obliging friend (or even a large cat!) may sit on a chair to weight it down in the correct position for one end, with the other end tied to the door knob.

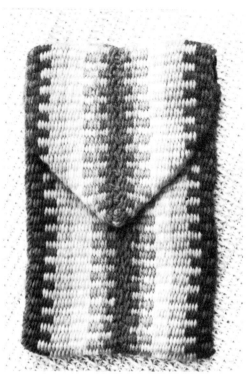

19. Pencil case from double width of braid.

As the warp is drawn up so closely, there are enough ends to finish off in fat cords or plaits, or the weft can be used to oversew across the braid, and the ends cut short.

If you are going to join braids side by side, you can plan one width of braid as half the pattern so that when joined it gives the appearance of a wide braid, as in the pencil case illustrated on page 54.

When making a button-hole band, or guitar strap, work the slits where required, taking the weft through one half of the warp, and working on this half until the slit is long enough, then breaking the weft and rejoining to work on the other half of the warp. When both sides are equal, work right across as before, weaving in the broken weft thread.

Anyone really interested in making braids will enjoy using an inkle loom, a simple frame, ready-made or home-made, enabling you to make wider, longer, and more complicated braids than would be convenient with a waist 'loom'.

Improvisations

Improvised Looms

Improvised weaving frames can be used when your frame loom is too small or not available. A clothes airing rack, or anything else with parallel bars – even a fence in warm weather – with one or two warp rods of suitable length, can be used as an upright loom.

Tie the warp rods to the top and bottom bars, with adjustable strings, and tie holding strings between the rods until the warp is in place.

Put on the warp, either in pairs or as a continuous warp. Put the shed stick in place, adding strings so that the stick is suspended from the top bar. If the reed is to be used, it will need to be hung from the top bar, too.

An improvised loom like this is useful for tapestry weaving, whether for small articles, like purses, or using heavier materials, for a wall hanging or stool top.

A 'free' weaving shape can be woven on an improvised loom. For instance, natural branches and twigs make good frames for imaginative weaving.

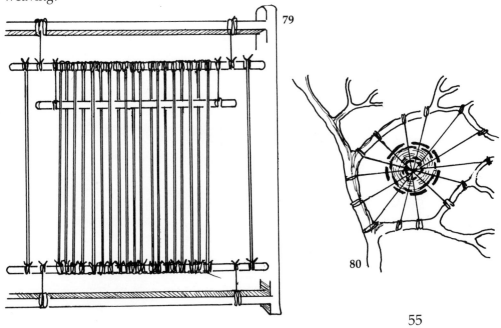

79

80

55

'Free' Weaving Shapes

A free shape, like the clown on the cover, can be woven on the frame loom or on an improvised frame without the reed.

A continuous warp makes it easy to spread the warp in different ways as the work progresses.

As you can see from the photograph of a partly woven clown, a shed stick is suspended from the top. Flat sticks are inserted in the part of the warp for the hat and hair, which are woven later. The face is worked first, going under and over two, to draw the warp in, using fairly fine wool and working the features tapestry style.

The neck ruff is Ghiordes knots, then for the top of the body (working under one, over one now), long loops are left at each side for finger weaving into arms later. Beyond this lines of chaining and soumak give a change of texture and help spread the warp, which is later divided for the legs.

After working Ghiordes knot ruffs, the warp is pulled in closely for the ankles and worked in needleweaving, the foot being worked on added loops after transferring the clown to his trapeze.

When the sticks are removed the hair is worked, then the warp loops are pushed together on the rod, so that the hat can be worked to a point, using a needle when it becomes difficult to use a shuttle. The remaining loop is transferred to the rod you choose for 'hanging' your clown.

81a

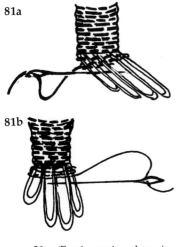

81b

20. 'Free' weaving shape in progress on improvised loom.

Finger weaving on very short lengths is awkward, so the arm loops are extended with oddments of wool, which are removed when the sleeve is finished. Then short loops are added as for the feet, and the hands are worked in needle weaving.

When the trapeze with its cord is completed the hands are stitched so that they are 'holding' the cord, and can be moved up and down.

The wrist ruffs are larkshead knots on a length of matching wool, tied round the wrist.

Lampshade rings as frames

Lampshade rings, or similar hoops, can be adapted in various ways as weaving frames. The warp threads stay in place if the ring is first worked around with crochet or buttonhole stitch, but if you want to slide part of the warp along the ring in the course of weaving, put the warp directly onto the ring, filling in any spaces later.

The warp may be fixed so that all the threads cross in the centre, as for the circular shapes in woven applique, or may be laid across in an irregular pattern, adding to the design as the work progresses.

Beads can be used to add interest, particularly if they are big enough to take several threads which can radiate in different directions.

By working part of the design in needle-weaving, then adding more warp threads which cross the worked part at a different angle, a double layer can be woven.

Try the effect of varying the spacing from very close to open weave, and leave some open warp threads. The resulting patterns can be used as mobiles, wall plaques, or, with suitable padding, as lids for work baskets.

How to use your Weaving

Shoulder Bag

A bag can be made from two pieces of weaving, matching in size and weight, although they do not need to be of the same pattern.

Knot the warp ends together to make a fringe along the bottom of the bag, or neaten each piece by running the ends back into the weaving.

Before sewing the bag, pin out and press, using a hot iron and damp cloth for wool, or a cooler iron for synthetic fibres.

A side pocket can be added, stitching it across the base, then joining it in with the side seams.

For the handle make a heavy four strand cord, a length of closely worked finger weaving, or for really hard wear, Norwegian braid. Make it long enough to cover the seams, reaching to the bottom of the bag, and stitch firmly, working from the right side.

Turn over the top to the inside and stitch firmly, or to the right side and cover it with braid, which can also be used as a strong, decorative finish for the top of a side pocket. This braid should go under the braid used for the gusset and handle.

82

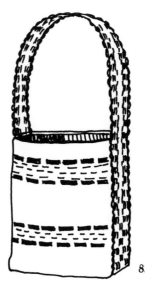

83

21. Bucket bag.

Bucket Bag

From a double length of weaving cut a piece for the base, oversewing the cut ends, and make the main part into a tube, which will fit round the base. Sew braid round the top, covering the join with the handle. This is stitched in place before sewing in the base, which is backstitched from the inside. Add a layer of stiffening in the base, and line the bag.

Purses

A purse made on a polystyrene frame, or on a continuous warp, is quickly finished off. A flap purse may be fastened with a button and loop, velcro, or press studs. Beads stitched to the flap hold it down without a fastening, if the purse hangs from a cord as a neck purse.

For a zip-fastened purse, start by making the lining, and stitch the zip to that, then when the side seams of the purse are finished, slip-stitch the edges of the weaving onto the zip tape. Add a tassel to the zip pull.

Neck straps of cord, braid, or finger weaving can be added, stitching firmly to the side seams.

Your weaving may also be fixed to ready-made purse frames.

Belts

Link fasteners are particularly useful for braid belts, as once fixed the ends are not disturbed. Size adjustment can be allowed for by fixing one end with a length of Velcro.

If one end of the braid is smoothly finished off, or enclosed in suede or lightweight leather, an ordinary buckle can be fixed.

A purse, with cord or braid loops across the back, can be added to your belt, as in the picture on page 53.

60

Sandals

Draw round your foot, or a pair of sandals of the right size, and from the pattern cut several thicknesses of strong fabric – old clothes will do – so that you have two piles about 1 cm deep. Include a stiff layer, like buckram, canvas, or lino. Stitch together, then cut an 'insole' to match your braid. Being careful to make a sole for each foot, stitch the top layer on with a binding strip, which is then turned over and stitched underneath.

Cut soles from leather oddments (available at most craft shops) but do not fix them yet.

Testing with oddments of fabric, or using old sandals as a guide, cut straps from braid and stitch and/or stick under the soles. Finally stick or stitch on the soles, putting extra layers at the heels, and adding bought stick-on soles if you wish. Ties of cord can be threaded through buttonholed loops.

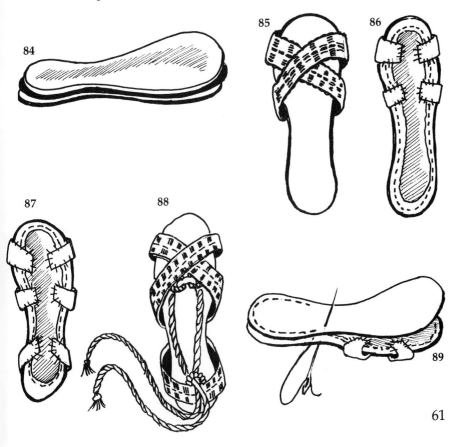

84

85

86

87

88

89

61

Weaving Terms Explained

Beat	— Push weft into place with reed, comb or fork.
Butterfly	— Weft wound round finger and thumb in a figure of eight, used instead of shuttle in tapestry weaving.
Chaining	— Loops worked round warp ends, like chain stitch in embroidery to space warp and produce a raised effect.
Continuous warp	—Warp made by taking a single thread round the warp bars from end to end, instead of tying separate warp threads.
Dent	— Space between two teeth in the reed.
Ends	— Individual warp threads.
Heddle	— Apparatus made to hold warp ends in order. The hole-and-slot heddle has alternate holes and slots, through which warp is threaded.
Plain weave	— Basic weave, of under one, over one alternating with over one, under one.
Reed	— A device with evenly spaced teeth to space the warp correctly and act as beater.
Selvedge	— The woven edge of the cloth.
Shed	— The V-shaped opening made when the warp is divided into two layers for the passage of the shuttle.
Shed sticks	— Sticks threaded through the shed behind the reed and/or heddle, keeping the threads in position.
Shot	— A single row of weft.
Shuttle	— A tool for carrying the weft.
Warp	— Lengthwise threads stretched on the loom.
Warp end bar	— The rod to which the warp ends are attached for weaving.
Weft	— The threads which interlace the warp, going across the cloth.

Useful Books

The Basic Book of Finger Weaving *Esther Warner Dendel* Nelson
Weaving Bands *Trotzig & Axelsson* Van Nostrand Reinhold
Inkle Loom Weaving *Frances B. Smith* Oak Tree Press
Introducing Weaving *Phyl Shillinglaw* Batsford
Off the Loom *Shirley Marein* Studio Vista
The Off Loom Weaving Book *Naumann & Hall* Pitman
Bead Threading and Bead Looming *Leisure Crafts No. 37* Search Press

Useful Addresses

Beads and Bead Looms	Hobby Horse, 15-17 Langton Street, London SW10
Beads and Bead Looms	Fred Aldous Ltd, 37 Lever Street, Manchester M60 1UX
Inkle Looms	E. T. Bradley, 82 North Lane, East Preston, Sussex BN16 1HE
Inkle Looms, Weaving Frames, Bead Looms, Table Looms, Weaving Accessories	Peter Elliott, 23 Croydon Road, Reigate, Surrey.
Spindles, Spinning Equipment, Tuition	The Handweavers' Studio 29 Haroldstone Road, London E17 7AN.

ACKNOWLEDGEMENTS

Colour photography by Terry Sims

Black and white photographs by Stephen
Hobden.

Doll (lower right p.56) by Linda Mosey

Drawings by Peggy Tasker

First published by Kaye & Ward Ltd
21 New Street, London EC2M 4NT
1979

ISBN 0 7182 1317 3

Set in VIP Palatino by
S. G. Mason (Chester) Ltd
**Printed and bound in Great Britain by
Cox & Wyman Ltd
London, Fakenham and Reading**